Sailing Vessels in Authentic Early Nineteenth-Century Illustrations

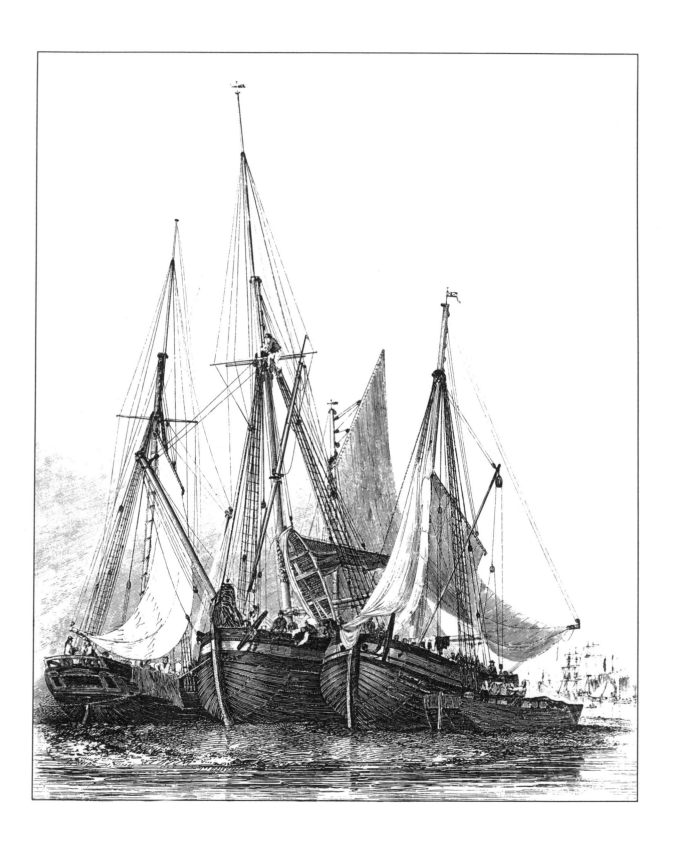

Sailing Vessels in Authentic Early Nineteenth-Century Illustrations

("Sixty Five Plates of Shipping and Craft")

BY

EDWARD WILLIAM COOKE

DOVER PUBLICATIONS, INC., New York

Copyright © 1989 by Dover Publications, Inc.
All rights reserved under Pan American and International Copyright Conventions.

Published in Canada by General Publishing Company, Ltd., 30 Lesmill Road, Don Mills, Toronto, Ontario.
Published in the United Kingdom by Constable and Company, Ltd.

This Dover edition, first published in 1989, is an unabridged, unaltered republication of the work originally published in London under the title *Sixty Five Plates of Shipping and Craft*. A Publisher's Note, written specially for the present edition, draws upon the Annual Lecture of the Society for Nautical Research [1966]: "E. W. Cooke, Marine Painter," by John Munday, as published in *Mariner's Mirror*, pp. 99–113, vol. 53, 1967.

The publisher gratefully acknowledges the cooperation of the Hart Nautical Collections, The MIT Museum, Cambridge, Massachusetts, in making its copy of the work available for reproduction.

DOVER *Pictorial Archive* SERIES

Manufactured in the United States of America
Dover Publications, Inc., 31 East 2nd Street, Mineola, N.Y. 11501

Library of Congress Cataloging-in-Publication Data

Cooke, Edward William, 1811–1880.
   [Sixty five plates of shipping and craft]
   Sailing vessels in authentic early nineteenth-century illustrations : sixty five plates of shipping and craft / by Edward William Cooke.
      p.   cm.
   Reprint. Originally published: Sixty five plates of shipping and craft. London, 1829.
   ISBN 0-486-26141-7
   1. Cooke, Edward William, 1811–1880. 2. Sailing ships in art. I. Title.
NC978.5.C66A4   1989
741.6′4′092—dc20   89-11923
                                                         CIP

Publisher's Note

EDWARD WILLIAM COOKE was born on March 27, 1811, in Pentonville, London. Many members of the family were artists: Edward's father, George (1781–1834), was a noted engraver of illustrations who, among other accomplishments, created many of the plates engraved from illustrations by J. M. W. Turner for *Picturesque Views on the Southern Coast of England* (1814–26). George's brother, William Bernard Cooke (1778–1855), also contributed many plates to the work.

Edward manifested his own artistic talent early, drawing and engraving botanical studies and, reportedly, studying perspective under Augustus Charles Pugin. He contributed plates to his father's *London and its Vicinity* (1820–34). Having an interest in shipping and maritime views, he studied ships under the guidance of Captain Burton of the *Thetis* (see p. 17).

In March 1828, Cooke published the first installment of *Fifty Plates of Shipping and Craft*, concentrating on the Thames and its river craft. Later installments also included plates depicting scenes of interest at Portsmouth and Brighton. In December 1829, on completion of the project, a title page was engraved. The work did not contain printed text. Subsequently, Cooke went on various sketching trips in Britain. He issued a prospectus for a series, "Coast Sketches," for which he completed several plates before abandoning the project. Similarly, an attempt at another series, "The British Coast," remained uncompleted after views of Kingsgate, Folkestone and Dover had been executed in 1831. These etchings, along with those for "Coast Sketches," were added to *Shipping and Craft*. The title page was corrected to *Sixty Five Plates of Shipping and Craft*, although the date, 1829, was left unaltered. In 1840, Cooke sold the plates and remaining sheets to Henry Bohn, who brought out his own edition.

Cooke's illustrations are notable for the accuracy of the details lavished on them, and the artist's ability to depict the effects of varying winds and waters on different types of craft. The book is a record of the age of sail as it was when steam was just beginning to make its effect felt.

Cooke executed some other graphic works, including *Views of the Old and the New London Bridges* (1833), but quickly shifted to painting in oil as his primary medium of expression. Making a specialty of marine views (notably those depicting the Dutch coasts), but also branching into Venetian and Egyptian scenes, he became a member of the Royal Academy, the British Institution and the Accademia delle Belle Arti (Venice). He enjoyed a long and successful career, although critics occasionally complained that he mined the same subjects too frequently and in excessive detail.

A typical Victorian in the range and diversity of his interests, Cooke belonged to the Alpine Club, the Institute of British Architects, the Linnaean Society and the Society of Antiquaries. His major interests, aside from his devotion to painting, included botany, horticulture, paleontology, geology and his collection of Venetian glass. He died on January 4, 1880.

NOTE: This edition reproduces the plates from an unbound copy of the work in the Hart Nautical Collections, The MIT Museum. (It is conceivable that the specific contents of other copies may vary to some extent.) The captions are adapted from the originals.

List of Plates

Sailing Vessels in Authentic Early Nineteenth-Century Illustrations

SIXTY FIVE PLATES

OF

SHIPPING

AND

CRAFT,

DRAWN AND ETCHED

BY

E. W. COOKE.

LONDON.

1829.

[Original title page.]

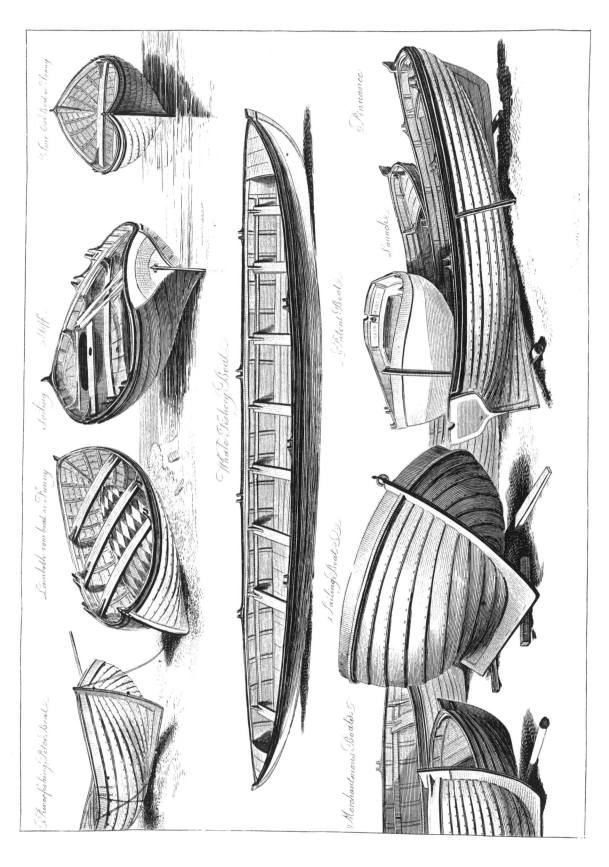

Four Oar'd Boat or Wherry

Skiff

Sculling

Lambeth row boat or Wherry

Whale Fishery Boat

River fishing Peter Boat

Sailing Boat

Merchantmen's Boats

Patent Boat

Launches

Pinnance

[Small boats.]

2

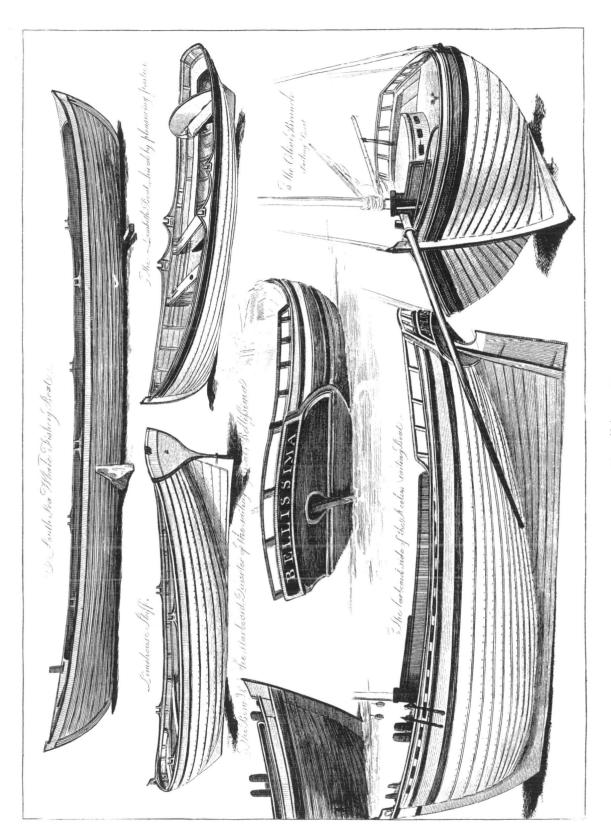

[Small boats.]

3

Yarmouth cobles, on the beach.

The *Thames*, East Indiaman, 1424 tons, built for, and employed by, the
Honourable East India Company. James Keith Forbes, commander.

Kemp-stairs, near Kingsgate.

Anchors.

Hay boats.

Scotch smacks.

Folkestone harbor, low water.

Billy-boy unloading at Shoreham harbor, low water.

Fishing smack.

Fishing boat.

Frigate.   Seventy-four.   Pilot boat.
                                              At Spithead.

Barge and canal boats.

Barque, free-trader, London docks.

First-class West Indiaman *Thetis* (Captain Burton) getting under
weigh off the Needles, Isle of Wight.

Prison ship in Portsmouth harbor, convicts going on board.

The *Discovery*, convict ship, lying at Deptford; the vessel that accompanied Captain Cook on his last voyage.

H.M.S. *Prince*, first-rate, 110 guns.

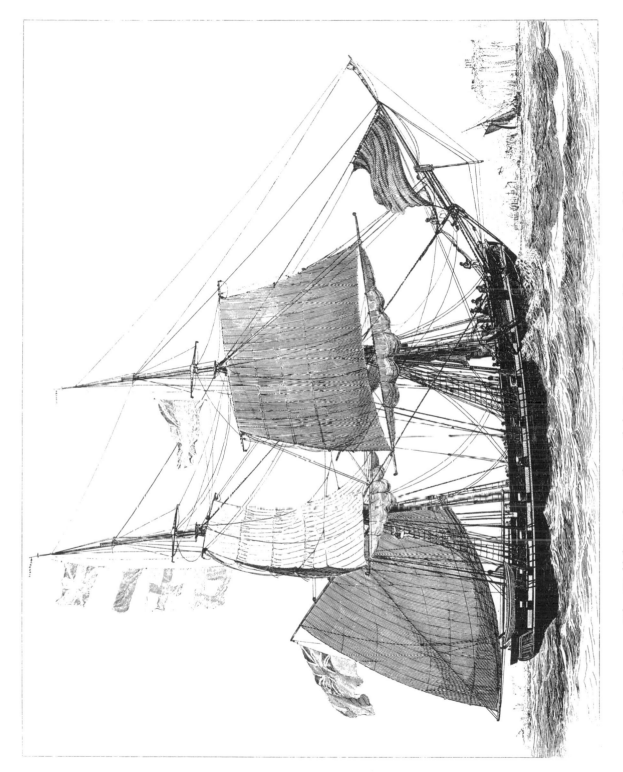

The *Wolf*, brig of war (late of the Royal Navy), making signal and laying to for a pilot off Dover.

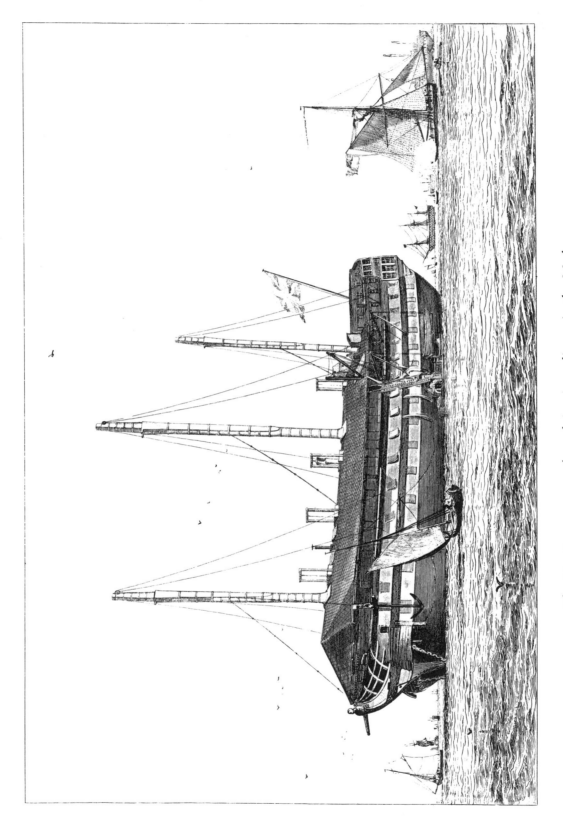

The *Hastings*, seventy-four, lying in ordinary in the Medway.

The *Victory*, first-rate, 104 guns, in Portsmouth harbor, 1828; collier alongside.

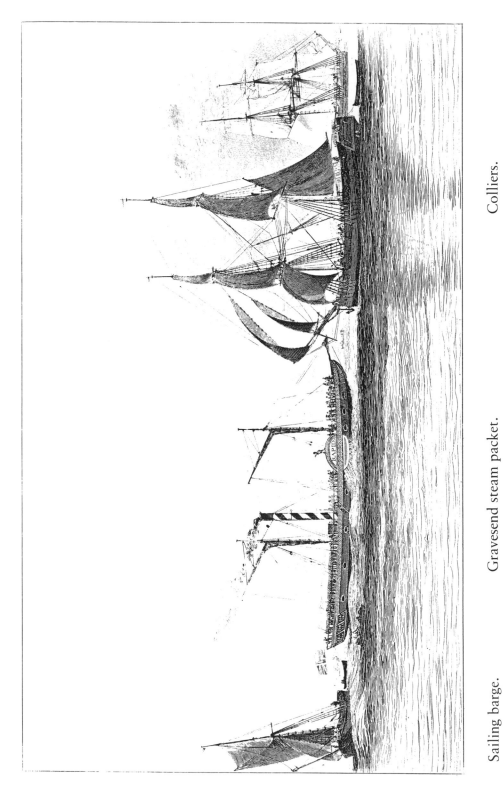

Colliers.

Gravesend steam packet.

Sailing barge.

24

The *United Kingdom* (Edinburgh), steam vessel, 1000 tons burden,
200 horsepower.

Hatch boat (double-reefed) off Gravesend.

Collier in a calm.

Yarmouth herring boat (lugger) unloading at the quay.

Brighton fishing boats on the beach.

Sailing barges.

The Stationers' Barge.

Lugger on the beach, Brighton.

Thames wherries, Richmond.

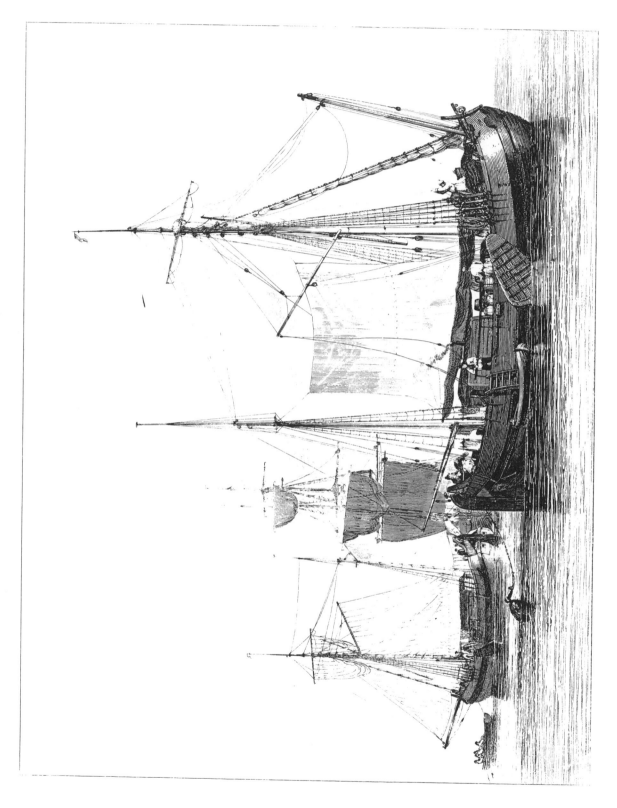

Dutch galliots.

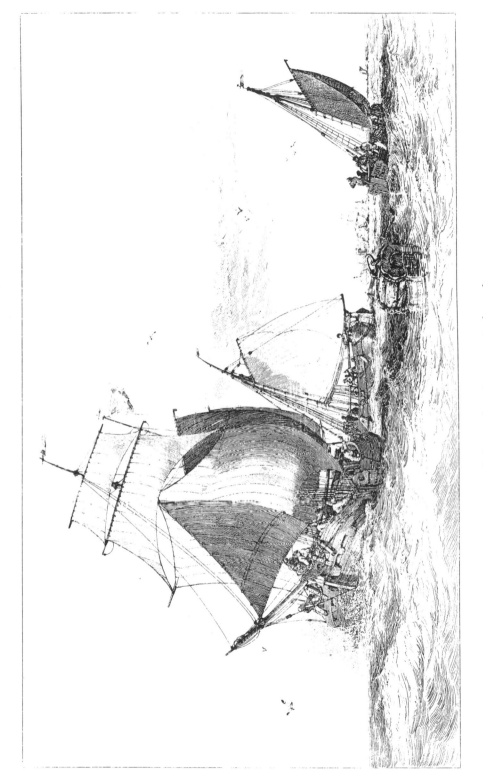

Dutch boats beating to windward.

4

Prawn boats, Brighton beach, April 1830.

Hog boats near the Battery, Brighton, May 1830.

Rope houses on the beach at Brighton.

Mackerel boats coming in, Brighton.

Thames barge going before the wind off Northfleet.

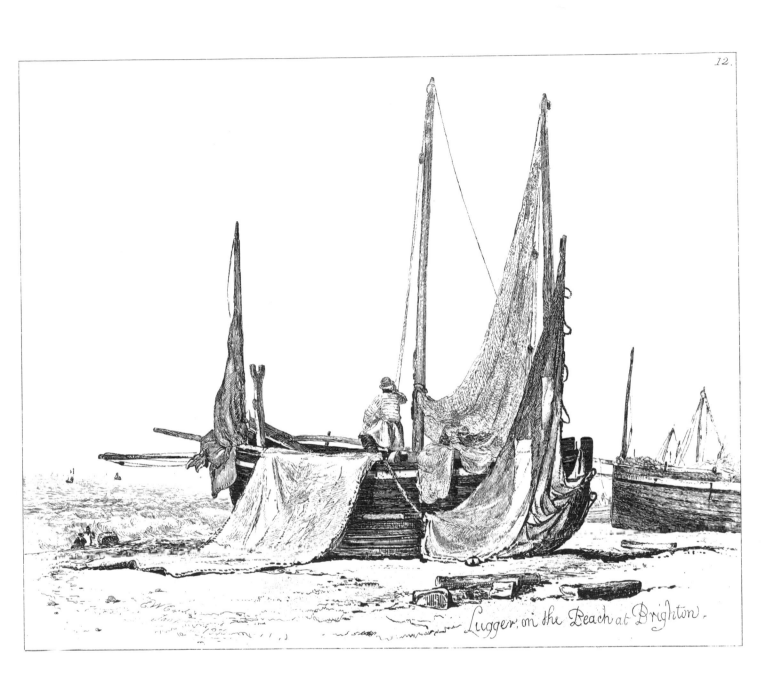

Lugger on the Beach at Brighton.

Lugger on the beach at Brighton.

Dutch galliot unloading, Great Yarmouth.

The circular stern of H.M.S. *Asia*, 84 guns, one of
the ships in the engagement at Navarino.

A brig of war's 12-pounder carronade.

Lugger near the blockade station, Brighton.

45

Sheer hulk in Portsmouth harbor.

Dutch schuyt, Blackwall Reach.

Prussian snow.

Frigate under all sail.

Skiff at the entrance to the West Indian docks, Blackwall.

50

On the beach at Cromer.

Cowes boat coming out of the harbor.

Fishing boat arrived.

Schooner and smack (coasting traders) lying at Fresh Wharf, London Bridge.

Mud dredger, Portsmouth harbor.

Lobster boat at Rottingdean.

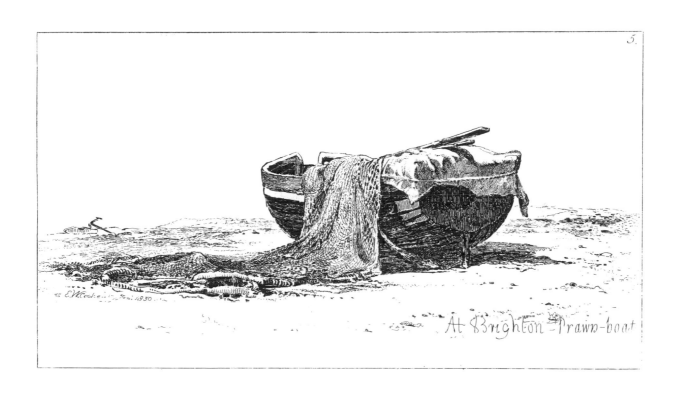

Prawn boat at Brighton.

Hog boat on the sands at Brighton.

Boat hut, Brighton beach.

Peter boats at Greenwich.

Crab boat at Rottingdean.

Oyster boats at Billingsgate.

Collier discharging.

Fishing smack.   Schooner.   Sloop-rigged barge.

Barges.